THELONIOUS MONK
EASY PIANO SOLOS

T0052809

Photo: Raymond Ross Photography, New York City

ISBN 978-0-7935-8759-9

HAL•LEONARD®
CORPORATION
7777 W. BLUEMOUND RD. P.O. BOX 13819 MILWAUKEE, WI 53213

Visit Hal Leonard Online at
www.halleonard.com

CONTENTS

BIOGRAPHY

For many years, misunderstood and criticized, the art of Thelonious Monk is now regarded as key when the evolution of jazz is discussed and chronicled.

He was born in Rocky Mount, North Carolina in 1917, and at the age of four, his family moved to New York. In his early twenties, Monk was already playing in various bands in the city, as well as participating in the jam sessions at Minton's Playhouse, the club where the earliest experiments in the music later called "bebop" occurred. He made his first recordings with Coleman Hawkins in 1944, and trumpeter/bandleader Cootie Williams recorded his song "'Round Midnight" that same year. Monk later joined Dizzy Gillespie's big band and continued to compose. In 1947, he began the first in a series of recordings for the Blue Note label, where his unusual compositions and playing style were first heard in their purest form. This important series ended in 1952. Although the records did not sell well during this period, many are now regarded as masterpieces.

Monk signed with Prestige Records in 1952, but his records sold so poorly that his contract was sold to Riverside Records in 1955. Although producer Orrin Keepnews initially had Monk record music by other composers, by the third album in the contract, Thelonious returned to playing his own music. By 1957, his career was in full swing, and his albums and club and television appearances were highly praised. He had John Coltrane in his group for a few months, and Coltrane later said that playing with Monk was a stimulating and educational experience (a private recording of the group performing at the Five Spot sold very well when it was made available in the early '90s). Another high point for Monk was his appearance with a tentet at New York's Town Hall (also recorded by Riverside) with arrangements by Hall Overton. In some of the arrangements, Overton transcribed and scored some of Monk's solos for the group.

By 1962, Monk had become such an important artist that Columbia Records signed him to a contract. His picture appeared on the cover of *Time* magazine in 1964, and he toured all over the world. Usually he played in a quartet setting, although during one important European tour, he played with an all-star octet. However, by 1970, he'd broken up his regular group and toured with the Giants of Jazz, which included Dizzy Gillespie, Sonny Stitt, Kai Winding, Al McKibbon and Art Blakey. After a few sporadic performances in the next few years, he retired by the end of the decade. He died at the home of his patron and friend Baroness Pannonica de Koenigswarter, in 1982.

Monk had a profound influence on jazz from the late forties onward. His pianistic approach, rooted in the stride style of Fats Waller and James P. Johnson, embraced modes, whole tones, clusters and polytonality. His compositions remain an important resource in the jazz repertoire, with many of his tunes now considered standards and part of every improvising musician's library. His music will continue to delight and challenge every serious jazz musician in decades to come.

PERFORMANCE NOTES

Writing easy piano arrangements of the compositions of Thelonious Monk poses many challenges to the arranger. Many of Monk's pieces sound simple, which is part of the challenge in learning them. Monk utilized familiar harmonic patterns in unusual ways, and his melodies are highly unpredictable. For these reasons, it is highly recommended that you listen to Monk play these pieces, and a discography of Monk performances can be found on page 38 of this folio. Please note that the composition "Two Timer" was never recorded by Monk; the recording listed in the discography is a band performance led by Monk's son, T.S. Monk.

Due to the many instances of complex harmony in these compositions, there are a number of times when chords are tricky to read. Leaving out notes to further simplify these pieces would rob them of the unique sound of Monk's style. Some chords in the left hand may have to be rolled to be played by those with small hands. In some instances, chordal cadenzas are included in the last bar engraved in cue size. These are optional, but desired, and can be mastered with a little practice.

"Misterioso" has a musical figure unique to Thelonious Monk that needs explanation. On the last chord of the piece, the note G is articulated before the other right-hand notes D and A♭. By beat three, the finger playing the G should lift, resulting in a momentary dissonance.

The Monk family is very pleased that these compositions are available in simplified form, and they hope that you enjoy learning and playing them.

ABOUT THE ARRANGER

Ronnie Mathews is not only recognized as an important interpreter of the music of Thelonious Monk; he is a gifted composer and pianist in his own right. Born in New York in 1935, he had completed three years of pre-med study at Brooklyn College when he began studying piano and composition with Hall Overton. He switched his major to music and obtained his degree in theory at the Manhattan School of Music. He has worked with Kenny Dorham, Max Roach, Freddie Hubbard, Dexter Gordon, Art Blakey, Woody Shaw and Johnny Griffin. He has made many recordings with a wide variety of jazz artists and under his own name. He currently plays in the T.S. Monk band, as well as making regular trips to Japan to concertize and record.

ASK ME NOW

By THELONIOUS MONK

BEMSHA SWING

By THELONIOUS MONK and DENZIL BEST

BLUE MONK

By THELONIOUS MONK

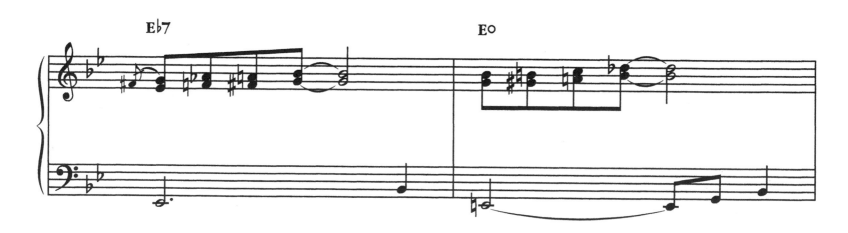

BYE-YA

By THELONIOUS MONK

Heavy Swing bass line

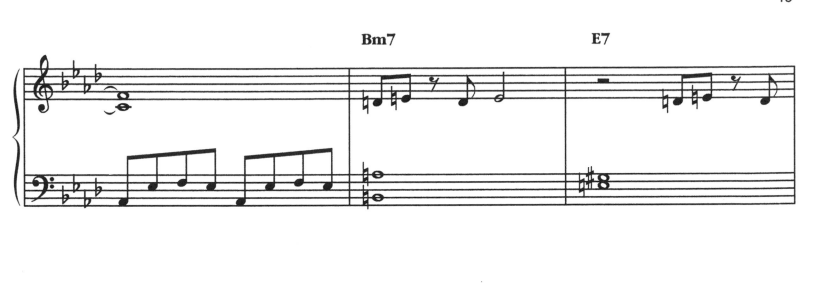

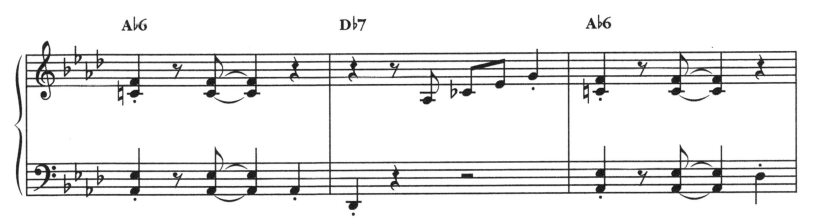

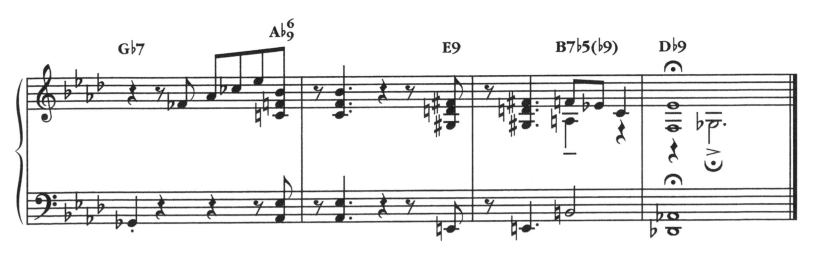

EVIDENCE

By THELONIOUS MONK

Medium up Swing
$\quad$ = ca.192

✳ This chord may have to be rolled.

I MEAN YOU

By THELONIOUS MONK and COLEMAN HAWKINS

JACKIE-ING

By THELONIOUS MONK

Medium Swing

$\stackrel{}{\rule{0pt}{0pt}} = \text{ca.}104$

LIGHT BLUE

By THELONIOUS MONK

LET'S COOL ONE

By THELONIOUS MONK

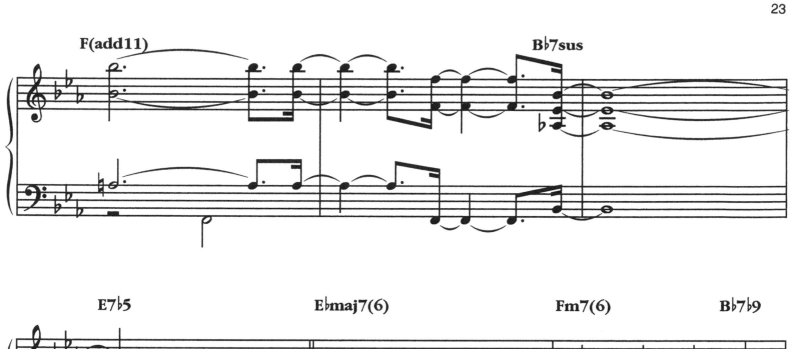

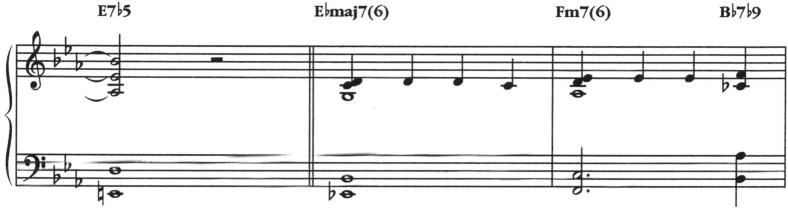

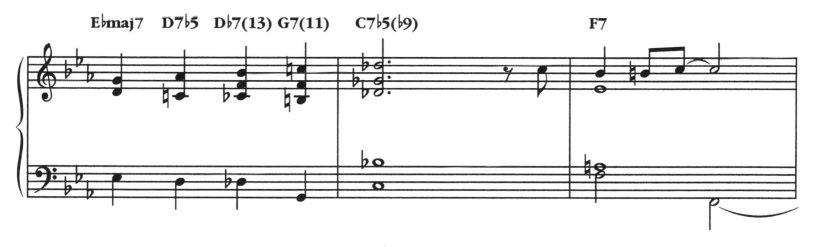

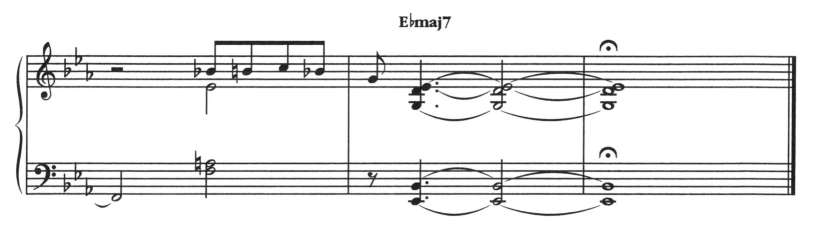

MISTERIOSO

By THELONIOUS MONK

Even eighths

$\quad \bullet$ = ca.66

✻ Strike G, then remove.

MONK'S DREAM

By THELONIOUS MONK

STRAIGHT, NO CHASER

By THELONIOUS MONK

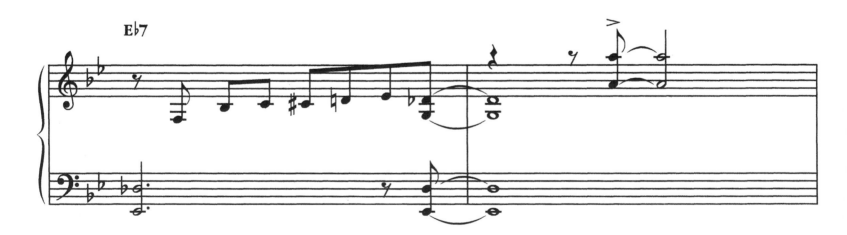

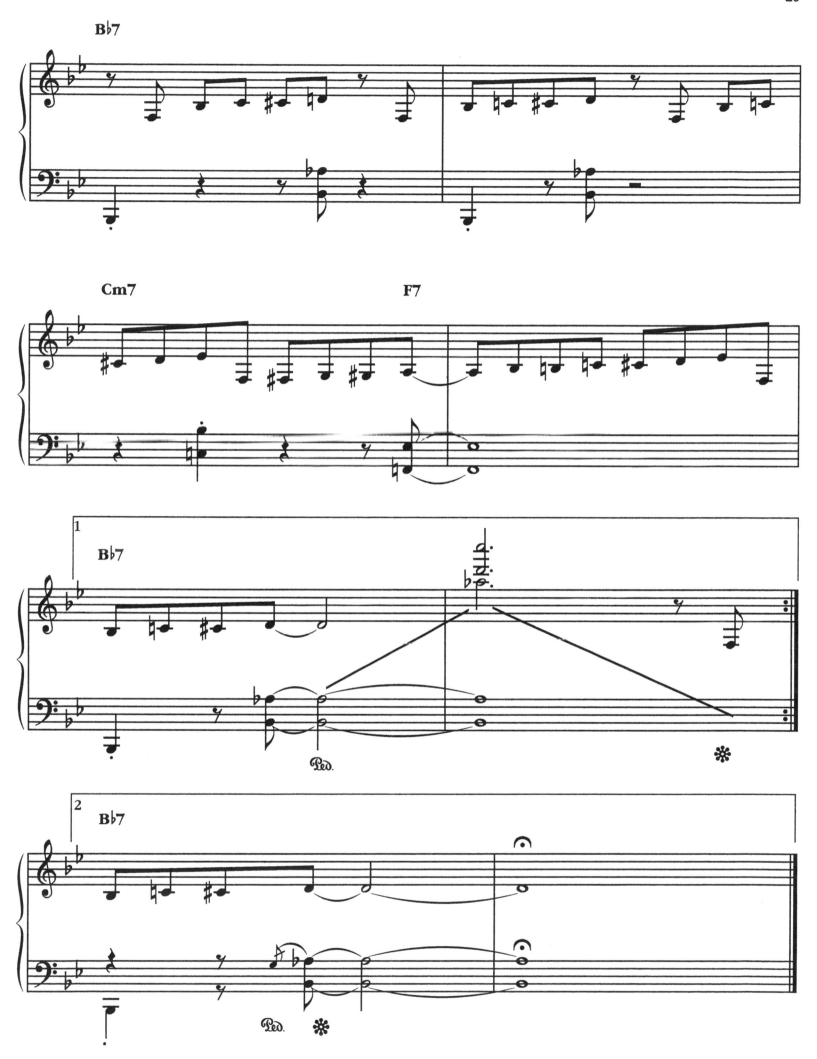

THINK OF ONE

By THELONIOUS MONK

Medium Swing

$\quad = \text{ca.}148$

TWO TIMER

By THELONIOUS MONK

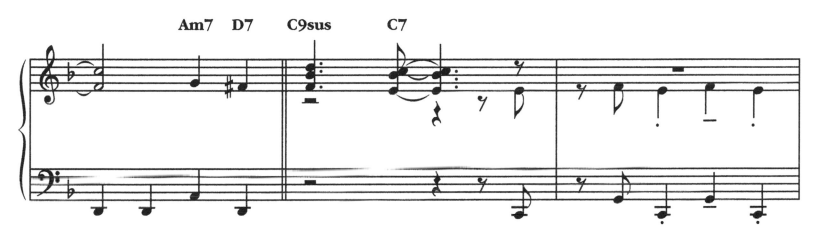

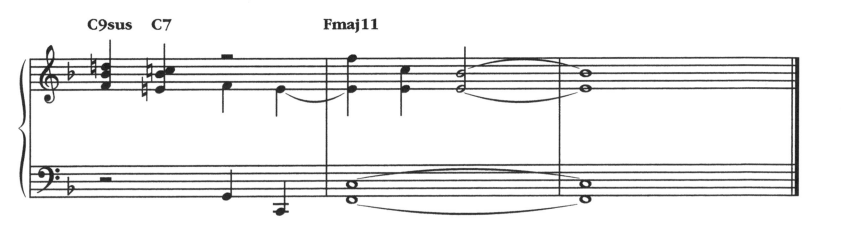

UGLY BEAUTY

By THELONIOUS MONK

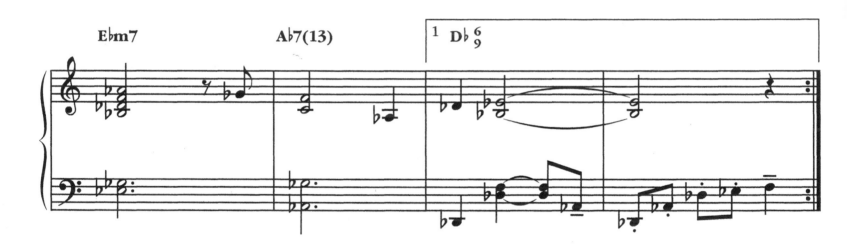

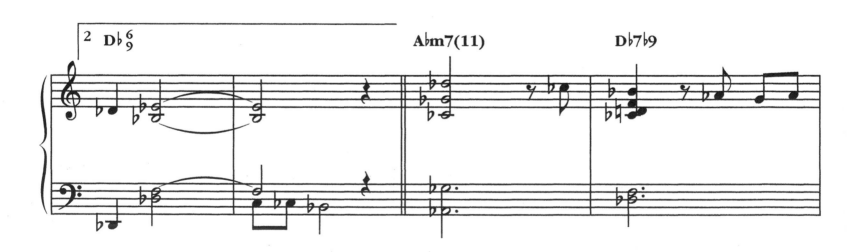

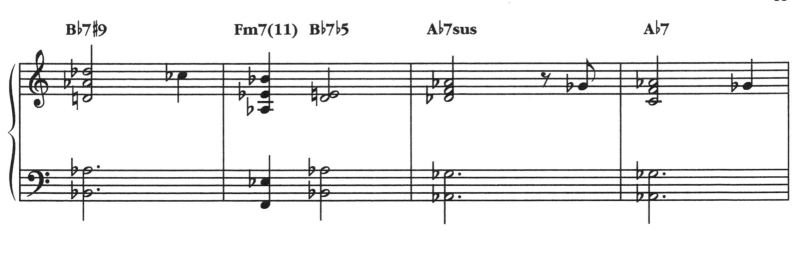

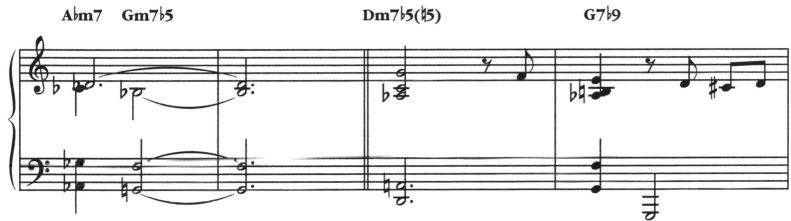

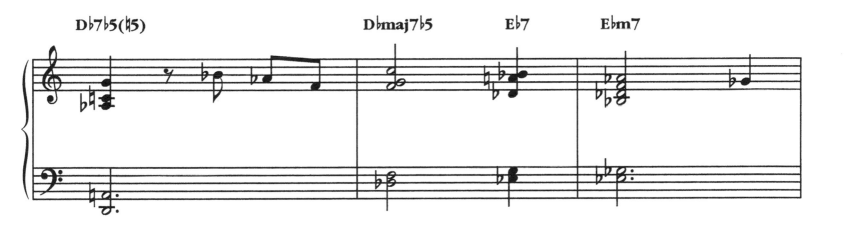

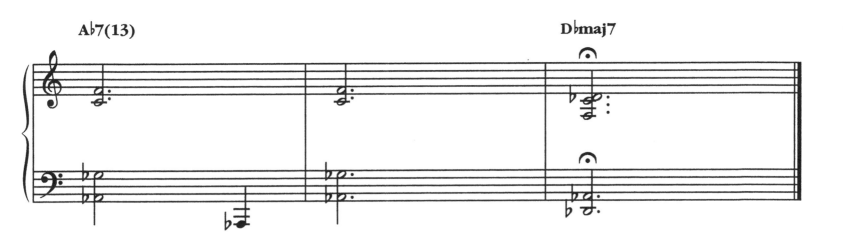

WE SEE

By THELONIOUS MONK

DISCOGRAPHY OF MONK PERFORMANCES

Thelonious Monk recorded his own compositions many times over the course of his career. The recordings cited are the earliest known Monk-performed studio recordings of these pieces. As stated in the performance notes, the composition "Two Timer" was not recorded by Thelonious. It appears on the CD *T.S. Monk By Monk* (N2K-N2KE 10017).

EVIDENCE; I MEAN YOU; MISTERIOSO (7/2/48)/ASK ME NOW; STRAIGHT, NO CHASER (7/23/51)/LET'S COOL ONE (5/30/52) - THE COMPLETE BLUE NOTE RECORDINGS - CD: BLUE NOTE 30363

BYE-YA, MONK'S DREAM (10/15/52), BEMSHA SWING (12/18/52), BLUE MONK (9/22/54) - THELONIOUS MONK TRIO - CD: OJC-010

THINK OF ONE (11/13/54), WE SEE (5/11/54) - MONK - CD: OJC-016

LIGHT BLUE (8/7/58) - THELONIOUS IN ACTION - CD: OJC-103

JACKIE-ING (6/4/59) - FIVE BY MONK BY FIVE - CD: OJC 362

UGLY BEAUTY (12/14/67) - UNDERGROUND - CD: COLUMBIA CK 40785